Quick & Easy Guide To Article Marketing

INTRODUCTION

Welcome to the "Quick & Easy Guide to Article Marketing" eBook, your essential companion to navigating the dynamic landscape of content promotion and online influence. In this digital age, where information is abundant and attention spans are fleeting, mastering the art of article marketing has become a vital skill for individuals and businesses alike.

This comprehensive eBook is meticulously crafted to provide you with a straightforward yet comprehensive understanding of the strategies, techniques, and tactics that drive successful article marketing campaigns. Whether you're a seasoned marketer aiming to refine your approach or a newcomer eager to make a mark, this guide caters to all levels of expertise.

Article marketing is more than just writing words; it's about crafting a narrative that resonates with your audience, elevating your brand's credibility, and strategically positioning your content for maximum exposure. With our step-by-step insights, you'll learn to create captivating content that not only captures attention but also drives meaningful engagement.

From ideation to distribution, we'll walk you through the entire process, revealing the secrets of crafting compelling headlines, structuring articles for impact, and leveraging reputable platforms to amplify your reach. Whether you're a business looking to expand your online footprint or an individual eager to establish thought leadership, the "Quick & Easy Guide to Article Marketing" eBook is your gateway to unlocking the true potential of your content. Embark on this journey with us, and let's transform your articles into powerful tools of connection and influence.

Index

"Quick & Easy Guide to Article Marketing" offers you 15 simple yet effective strategies to excel in the realm of content promotion and online influence. This comprehensive resource equips you with actionable insights to effortlessly enhance your article marketing game. Here are the 15 ways it empowers you:

1. Strategic Ideation: Discover methods to generate impactful article ideas tailored to your target audience.

2. Compelling Content Creation: Learn to craft articles that resonate, inform, and captivate your readers.

3. Attention-Grabbing Headlines: Master the art of creating headlines that instantly pique curiosity and drive clicks.

4. Structural Brilliance: Explore techniques for organizing your articles to keep readers engaged from start to finish.

5. Keyword Optimization: Uncover how to seamlessly incorporate keywords for improved search engine visibility.

6. Audience Targeting: Pinpoint your ideal readership and tailor your content to meet their needs.

7. Platform Selection: Navigate various platforms to choose the right ones for publishing and distributing your articles.

8. Effective Outreach: Develop strategies to collaborate with influencers and other writers for extended reach.

9. Visual Enhancement: Learn to incorporate visuals that amplify the impact and understanding of your content.

10. Social Media Integration: Understand how to leverage social platforms to promote and share your articles.

11. Analytics Utilization: Harness the power of data to refine your strategies and optimize your article marketing approach.

12. Building Credibility: Establish yourself as an authority in your niche through well-researched and insightful articles.

13. Long-Term Engagement: Cultivate a loyal readership by consistently delivering value through your articles.

14. SEO Mastery: Implement advanced SEO techniques to improve your articles' visibility in search engines.

15. Measuring Success: Learn how to gauge the effectiveness of your article marketing efforts and make data-driven improvements.

"Quick & Easy Guide to Article Marketing" empowers you with these 15 strategies, allowing you to harness the full potential of your articles and make a significant impact in the online world.

Chapter <1>

Strategic Ideation: Unleashing Impactful Article Ideas Tailored to Your Audience

In the ever-evolving landscape of content creation, the art of strategic ideation stands as the foundation of successful article marketing. The process of generating compelling article ideas tailored precisely to your target audience is akin to crafting a blueprint for engagement, reach, and influence. In this comprehensive exploration, "Strategic Ideation: Unleashing Impactful Article Ideas Tailored to Your Audience," we delve into the depths of ideation techniques that will set you on a path to content creation mastery.

Understanding that each article is a gateway to capturing the attention of your readers, we embark on a journey that transforms mere concepts into captivating narratives. At the core of this process lies the recognition that resonating with your audience starts with knowing them intimately. We navigate through the multifaceted landscape of audience segmentation, leveraging demographics, psychographics, and behavioural patterns to create a robust foundation for ideation.

Diving deeper, we unearth methods that transcend the mundane and venture into the realm of innovation. The synthesis of ideas from disparate domains, the exploration of trending topics, and the identification of gaps in existing content form the stepping stones to crafting articles that stand out amidst the digital noise. Through real-world examples and expert insights, we illustrate how to fuse creativity with relevance, ensuring that each article resonates profoundly with its intended readers.

As the ideation process unfolds, the eBook unveils strategies for tapping into the collective intelligence of your team or community. Collaborative brainstorming sessions, crowdsourcing ideas, and engaging in vibrant discussions all play a pivotal role in enriching your content reservoir. With a host of tools and platforms at your disposal, you'll learn to harness the power of technology to refine and elevate the ideation process.

Intricately woven into the fabric of strategic ideation is the concept of solving problems and addressing pain points. By identifying the challenges faced by your audience, you'll not only create relevant content but also position yourself as a problem-solving authority. Case studies and anecdotes demonstrate how empathy-driven content can foster a deeper connection with readers, inspiring them to engage and share.

The journey continues with the exploration of diverse content formats. From informative how-to guides to thought-provoking opinion pieces, the eBook navigates through a plethora of options to showcase how tailoring your content to different formats can amplify its impact. Engaging visuals, infographics, and multimedia elements emerge as indispensable tools, enabling you to convey complex ideas with clarity and elegance.

Moreover, the eBook uncovers the secrets of evergreen content—articles that stand the test of time. By understanding the principles of timeless relevance and crafting content with enduring value, you'll establish a repository of articles that continue to attract and engage readers long after their publication. This not only cements your authority but also forms a cornerstone of your content marketing strategy.

The digital realm thrives on trends, and staying ahead of the curve is essential for sustained engagement. The eBook delves into the art of trendspotting, teaching you how to identify emerging topics and align your content with the zeitgeist. By doing so, you'll position yourself as a forward-thinking influencer, consistently providing content that resonates with the present while anticipating the future.

As the eBook draws to a close, it reinforces the symbiotic relationship between ideation and iteration. The journey from concept to completion is marked by continuous refinement, guided by analytics, feedback loops, and a commitment to learning. With a treasure trove of strategies for effective ideation, you'll be equipped to perpetually evolve and adapt your content creation approach.

"Strategic Ideation: Unleashing Impactful Article Ideas Tailored to Your Audience" is more than a guide; it's a transformative journey that equips you with the tools to navigate the creative landscape with finesse. Whether you're a seasoned content creator seeking to revitalise your approach or a novice venturing into the world of article marketing, this eBook empowers you to ideate with purpose, create with impact, and connect with authenticity. Embark on this enlightening expedition and elevate your article marketing strategy to unprecedented heights.

Chapter <2>

Compelling Content Creation: Crafting Articles that Resonate, Inform, and Captivate Your Readers

In the realm of article marketing, the craft of compelling content creation reigns supreme, acting as the linchpin between your ideas and your audience's engagement. "Compelling Content Creation: Crafting Articles that Resonate, Inform, and Captivate Your Readers" delves deep into the art and science of crafting articles that not only grab attention but also leave an indelible impact on your readers' minds.

At the heart of this exploration is the understanding that articles are vessels of communication, conduits that bridge the gap between your insights and the reader's understanding. The journey begins with an exploration of resonance—the profound connection that occurs when your content strikes a chord with your target audience. Through vivid anecdotes and practical strategies, we guide you in aligning your content with your audience's values, aspirations, and pain points, creating an emotional resonance that lingers long after reading.

An integral facet of compelling content creation is the seamless fusion of information and engagement. We delve into the techniques of infusing your articles with valuable insights, backed by thorough research and credible sources. This not only establishes your authority but also equips your readers with actionable takeaways, transforming your articles into reservoirs of knowledge.

Central to this journey is the concept of storytelling—a timeless art that humanizes your content and ignites imagination. The eBook navigates through the realms of narrative structure, character development, and emotional arcs, showcasing how weaving stories into your articles can cultivate a sense of relatability and empathy. By harnessing the power of storytelling, you'll be able to convey complex ideas in a relatable and memorable manner.

Moreover, the eBook unveils the architecture of impactful introductions and conclusions. These twin pillars of your article provide the first impression and the lasting resonance. We guide you through strategies to craft attention-grabbing openings that compel readers to journey further.

Similarly, we delve into methods to create conclusions that leave a lasting impression, inspiring readers to reflect, engage, and share.

The exploration wouldn't be complete without delving into the nuances of tone and voice. Whether you aim for an authoritative, conversational, or inspirational tone, we empower you with insights to maintain consistency and authenticity throughout your content. This fosters a connection with your audience, creating a sense of familiarity and trust that's essential for sustained engagement.

Visual engagement emerges as another cornerstone, and the eBook demystifies the integration of images, videos, and graphics into your articles. We showcase how visual elements can enhance understanding, convey emotions, and complement your narrative. From choosing the right visuals to ensuring accessibility, you'll learn to wield visuals as potent tools for enriching your content.

Furthermore, the eBook illuminates the art of structure and flow. Through templates and best practices, you'll learn to structure your articles for maximum readability and impact. Cohesive transitions, logical organisation, and effective signposts guide your readers seamlessly through your content, ensuring they remain immersed in your narrative.

As the journey unfolds, we delve into the art of addressing objections and counter arguments. By proactively acknowledging and addressing opposing viewpoints, you'll showcase intellectual honesty and strengthen your credibility. This approach not only fosters meaningful dialogue but also positions you as a thought leader open to discussion.

The eBook culminates with an exploration of engagement catalysts—strategies that prompt readers to take action. Whether it's inviting comments, encouraging social sharing, or suggesting follow-up reading, these catalysts nurture a vibrant community around your content.

This, in turn, fuels your influence and fosters a sense of connection with your readers.

"Compelling Content Creation: Crafting Articles that Resonate, Inform, and Captivate Your Readers" is more than a guide; it's a voyage through the intricacies of content creation, offering a roadmap to crafting articles that resonate on intellectual, emotional, and personal levels. Whether you're a seasoned wordsmith seeking to refine your approach or a novice embarking on your content creation journey, this eBook equips you with the tools to craft articles that inspire, inform, and leave a lasting imprint in the digital landscape. Join us on this transformative expedition and unleash the full potential of your content creation prowess.

Chapter <3>

Attention-Grabbing Headlines: Crafting Curiosity-Piquing Click Magnets

In a digital world overflowing with content, mastering the art of attention-grabbing headlines has become a pivotal skill.
"Attention-Grabbing Headlines: Crafting Curiosity-Piquing Click Magnets" takes you on a journey into the realm of headline creation, where language and psychology converge to entice readers, awaken curiosity, and drive clicks.

Understanding that a headline is your content's first impression, this exploration delves into the intricate mechanics that govern a reader's split-second decision to click or scroll past. By unravelling the psychology of what compels us to engage, we lay the groundwork for headline mastery.

The journey begins with the exploration of curiosity—an innate human drive that propels us to seek knowledge and solve mysteries. Through compelling examples and expert insights, we uncover techniques to infuse your headlines with just enough information to spark curiosity without revealing the entirety of the story. This delicate balance encourages readers to take the plunge and explore the article's depths.

Furthermore, the eBook illuminates the power of specificity—an art that distils your content's essence into a concise yet impactful headline. By offering a clear promise of what readers will gain from your article, you establish trust and transparency, setting the stage for a rewarding reading experience.

Venturing deeper, we dive into the realm of emotion-driven headlines. Harnessing readers' emotional responses—be it joy, empathy, fear, or excitement—creates an immediate connection, leading to increased engagement and sharing. We dissect emotional triggers and offer strategies to resonate with your audience's feelings, crafting headlines that resonate deeply.

Urgency emerges as another potent element, urging readers to act swiftly. Through urgency-driven headlines, you kindle a sense of immediacy, compelling readers to seize the moment and engage. By embracing the language of urgency, you tap into the fear of missing out and prompt immediate action.

Integral to this journey is the alignment between headline and content. Your headline serves as a promise, and delivering on that promise within your content is vital for reader retention and credibility. The eBook highlights the importance of coherence between the expectations set by the headline and the actual substance of the article.

Navigating through the nuances of language, we explore word choice, imagery, and rhythm as tools for headline creation. These elements shape the reader's perception and determine whether your headline resonates across diverse audiences.

The eBook also emphasises the iterative nature of headline creation. A/B testing allows you to compare different headlines and measure their effectiveness. This data-driven approach enables constant refinement, enhancing your ability to create headlines that consistently capture attention.

As the journey concludes, the eBook underscores ethical considerations in headline creation. Honesty and transparency are paramount, building trust and credibility with your audience. Ethical headlines not only ensure reader satisfaction but also nurture a lasting bond.

"Attention-Grabbing Headlines: Crafting Curiosity-Piquing Click Magnets" transcends traditional guides—it's a transformative odyssey into the fusion of language and psychology. Whether you're an experienced wordsmith seeking to elevate your headline skills or a newcomer navigating the realm of digital content, this eBook equips you with the tools to craft headlines that intrigue, captivate, and enthral. Join us on this immersive voyage and unlock the full potential of headline mastery, igniting curiosity and driving clicks in the digital landscape.

Chapter <4>

Structural Brilliance: Crafting Engaging Article Frameworks for End-to-End Reader Immersion

In the expansive realm of content creation, the significance of structural brilliance cannot be overstated. "Structural Brilliance: Crafting Engaging Article Frameworks for End-to-End Reader Immersion" takes you on a journey through the intricate art of organising your articles to captivate readers' attention from the very beginning and keep them engaged until the final word.

Understanding that the structure of an article is the roadmap to reader immersion, this exploration delves into the psychology and techniques that underscore an effective framework. We unravel the multifaceted layers that comprise an article's structural brilliance, paving the way for a comprehensive understanding of how to craft content that resonates deeply.

The journey commences by unveiling the power of a compelling introduction—a gateway that entices readers to venture further. Through vivid examples and expert insights, we demonstrate techniques to grab readers' attention with an opening that resonates emotionally, presents a challenge, or poses a question that demands exploration.

As the narrative unfolds, we delve into the significance of a coherent and logical flow. The eBook illuminates strategies to connect ideas seamlessly, ensuring that readers effortlessly transition from one section to another. A well-structured article is akin to a captivating story, with each section contributing to the overarching narrative while holding its own unique allure.

Central to the exploration is the concept of subheadings—a tool that guides readers through your content's labyrinth. We showcase how carefully crafted subheadings act as signposts, enabling readers to navigate the article's terrain with ease. By providing glimpses of what's to come, you set expectations while stoking curiosity.

Furthermore, the eBook unravels the art of the inverted pyramid—an age-old journalistic technique that places the most critical information at the article's outset. This approach caters to readers with varying levels of engagement, ensuring that even skimmers glean the core essence while those seeking depth find it in subsequent sections.

Intricately woven into the narrative is the concept of storytelling—a thread that weaves emotional engagement throughout your article. We explore techniques for incorporating anecdotes, case studies, and narratives that captivate readers on an intellectual and emotional level, fostering a profound connection.

Moreover, the eBook uncovers the significance of visual engagement. Images, infographics, and multimedia elements enrich the reading experience, breaking up text and providing visual reinforcement. We showcase how visuals complement the written word, enhancing comprehension and engagement.

The journey continues with the exploration of dynamic formatting. Short paragraphs, bullet points, and numbered lists enhance readability, making your content digestible and inviting. By incorporating whitespace strategically, you create a sense of balance and guide the reader's eye smoothly.

As the article nears its conclusion, the eBook delves into the art of crafting impactful conclusions. We provide insights into creating a sense of closure, leaving readers with a lasting impression or a call to action that encourages engagement beyond the article.

The eBook also highlights the role of audience-centricity in structural brilliance. By understanding your readers' preferences, habits, and pain points, you can tailor your article's structure to cater to their needs and keep them engaged.

"**Structural Brilliance:** Crafting Engaging Article Frameworks for End-to-End Reader Immersion" is not merely a guide—it's a transformative expedition through the intricate terrain of content organisation. Whether you're a seasoned writer aiming to refine your approach or a novice navigating the art of article creation, this eBook equips you with the tools to structure your content with finesse, guiding readers on a journey of continuous engagement. Join us on this immersive voyage and unlock the full potential of your article frameworks, fostering reader immersion from start to finish in the dynamic landscape of digital content.

Chapter <5>

Keyword Optimization: Seamlessly Integrating Keywords for Enhanced Search Engine Visibility

In the realm of digital content, where search engines act as the gateway to audience discovery, mastering keyword optimization is an indispensable skill. "**Keyword Optimization:** Seamlessly Integrating Keywords for Enhanced Search Engine Visibility" takes you on a journey through the intricacies of weaving keywords into your content to improve search engine rankings and increase visibility.

Understanding that keywords are the bridge connecting your content to its intended audience, this exploration delves into the strategic deployment of keywords, offering insights and techniques to ensure that your content not only resonates with readers but also aligns with the algorithms that power search engines.

The journey begins by demystifying the anatomy of keywords. We explore the nuances of short-tail and long-tail keywords, shedding light on their respective roles and impact. Armed with this understanding, you'll be equipped to choose keywords that strike a balance between search volume and specificity, driving both traffic and relevance.

Navigating deeper, the eBook unveils the significance of keyword research—a process that forms the cornerstone of effective optimization. We guide you through the tools and strategies required to identify high-performing keywords within your niche. By understanding user intent and gauging competition, you'll be empowered to select keywords that resonate with your target audience.

Furthermore, the eBook delves into the art of keyword placement. We showcase how to seamlessly integrate keywords into your content's structure, creating a natural and organic flow. From headlines and subheadings to body text and meta descriptions, every element of your content can be optimised to enhance search engine visibility without compromising readability.

The journey continues with the exploration of semantic search. As search engines evolve, they increasingly understand the context and intent behind user queries. We delve into the world of semantic keywords—terms related to your primary keywords—and reveal how incorporating them enriches your content's depth and relevance.

Moreover, the eBook uncovers the art of avoiding keyword stuffing—a practice that once promised rewards but now incurs penalties from search engines. We provide strategies for maintaining a healthy keyword density, ensuring that your content remains reader-friendly and aligned with search engine guidelines.

Intricately woven into the narrative is the significance of user experience. Search engines reward content that addresses readers' needs, and this eBook showcases how keyword optimization is inherently tied to providing value. By creating informative, engaging, and relevant content, you not only cater to your audience but also bolster your search engine ranking.

The journey extends to the world of content promotion. We explore how keyword optimization is instrumental in elevating your content's shareability and discoverability across platforms. Whether through social media, guest posting, or collaborations, optimised content becomes a magnet for engagement and visibility.

As the journey unfolds, we delve into the symbiotic relationship between keyword optimization and analytics. By tracking your content's performance, you can glean insights into keyword effectiveness and audience engagement. This data-driven approach empowers you to iterate and refine your optimization strategies continually.

"Keyword Optimization: Seamlessly Integrating Keywords for Enhanced Search Engine Visibility" transcends conventional guides—it's a transformative odyssey through the intersection of language, user intent, and search algorithms. Whether you're a seasoned content creator looking to amplify your reach or a newcomer navigating the intricacies of digital visibility, this eBook equips you with the tools to infuse your content with keywords that resonate and rank. Join us on this immersive journey and unlock the full potential of keyword optimization, propelling your content to the forefront of search engine visibility in the dynamic landscape of online discovery.

Chapter <6>

Audience Targeting: Crafting Tailored Content to Enrich Your Ideal Readers' Experience

In the vast and dynamic world of content creation, audience targeting stands as a compass guiding your content's trajectory towards meaningful engagement. "Audience Targeting: Crafting Tailored Content to Enrich Your Ideal Readers' Experience" embarks on a journey through the intricacies of identifying and captivating your ideal readers, ensuring that every piece of content resonates deeply and fosters lasting connections.

Understanding that content is a bridge between your ideas and your audience's needs, this exploration delves into the multifaceted process of audience targeting, equipping you with insights and strategies to not only attract but also captivate and retain your readers.

The journey commences by unravelling the significance of audience segmentation. We delve into the demographics, psychographics, and behavioural patterns that define your ideal readers. By painting a vivid picture of your target audience, you'll be empowered to create content that speaks directly to their preferences, interests, and pain points.

As the narrative unfolds, we explore the profound connection between empathy and content creation. The eBook showcases how walking in your audience's shoes—understanding their challenges, aspirations, and questions—enables you to craft content that addresses their needs directly. By resonating emotionally, you transform your content into a solution-driven companion for your readers.

Furthermore, the eBook unveils the art of crafting audience personas. These fictional representations of your ideal readers provide a tangible framework for content creation. We guide you through the process of creating detailed personas, offering insights into their goals, values, and media consumption habits. Armed with these personas, you can tailor your content to deliver maximum value.

The journey continues with the exploration of keyword research from an audience-centric perspective. We showcase how understanding your readers' search queries allows you to optimise your content for the very phrases they use. By aligning your keywords with your audience's language, you enhance the likelihood of your content appearing in their search results.

Moreover, the eBook delves into the significance of audience feedback. Listening to your readers—whether through comments, surveys, or social media interactions—provides invaluable insights into their preferences and expectations. We showcase how this feedback loop can refine your content strategy and ensure that your content continues to meet evolving needs.

Intricately woven into the narrative is the concept of content personalization. We explore how data-driven insights can fuel tailored content experiences. Whether through dynamic content recommendations or personalised email campaigns, you'll discover how to provide readers with content that feels tailor-made for them.

The journey extends to the realm of content format and delivery. Different readers engage with content in various ways, whether through articles, videos, podcasts, or infographics. We delve into how understanding your audience's preferred content formats allows you to diversify your offerings and cater to their consumption habits.

As the journey unfolds, we delve into the synergy between storytelling and audience engagement. By weaving relatable stories that mirror your readers' experiences, you create a bridge between your insights and their emotions. Through storytelling, your content becomes a vehicle for empathy, connection, and meaningful engagement.

"Audience Targeting: Crafting Tailored Content to Enrich Your Ideal Readers' Experience" transcends traditional guides—it's a transformative voyage through the realms of understanding, empathy, and connection. Whether you're a seasoned content creator aiming to refine your approach or a newcomer navigating the landscape of reader engagement, this eBook equips you with the tools to create content that deeply resonates with your audience. Join us on this immersive journey and unlock the full potential of audience targeting, forging lasting connections and enriching your readers' experience in the dynamic landscape of content creation.

Chapter <7>

Platform Selection: Navigating the Digital Landscape for Optimal Article Publishing and Distribution

In the fast-evolving realm of content distribution, platform selection has emerged as a strategic cornerstone for achieving maximum visibility and engagement. "Platform Selection: Navigating the Digital Landscape for Optimal Article Publishing and Distribution" invites you on a journey through the intricate process of choosing the right platforms to publish and share your articles, ensuring that your content reaches the right audience in the right way.

Understanding that each platform has its unique ecosystem and audience, this exploration delves into the art of platform selection, equipping you with insights and strategies to make informed decisions that align with your content goals and target readers.

The journey begins by acknowledging the diversity of platforms at your disposal. From social media giants to niche-specific forums, each platform offers a distinct avenue for content distribution. We unveil the power of research, highlighting the importance of understanding your audience's preferences and habits on each platform.

Navigating deeper, the eBook delves into the concept of audience overlap. By identifying platforms where your target readers congregate, you amplify the potential for engagement. Through real-world examples and expert insights, you'll uncover techniques to pinpoint the platforms that resonate most with your content.

Furthermore, the eBook explores the alignment between platform and content format. Different platforms cater to different content types—articles, videos, infographics, podcasts. We showcase how adapting your content to suit the strengths of each platform enhances its appeal and encourages sharing.

The journey continues with the exploration of platform demographics. Each platform hosts a diverse audience with specific demographics, interests, and behaviours. We provide insights into how understanding these nuances empowers you to tailor your content and approach, ensuring resonance with the platform's users.

Moreover, the eBook unveils the significance of platform culture. Every platform has its own unique tone, style, and etiquette. By immersing yourself in the culture of each platform, you position yourself as a valuable contributor rather than a mere promoter. This approach fosters authenticity and nurtures engagement.

Intricately woven into the narrative is the exploration of engagement dynamics. Some platforms thrive on conversations and discussions, while others focus on visual storytelling. We delve into strategies to engage effectively within each platform's context, fostering meaningful interactions that resonate with users.

The journey extends to the concept of consistency. Consistent posting and engagement are crucial for maintaining a presence on any platform. We provide insights into crafting a content calendar that aligns with each platform's algorithms and user behaviour, ensuring a steady stream of content that sustains engagement.

As the journey unfolds, we delve into the analytics-driven approach to platform selection. Monitoring metrics like reach, engagement, and click-through rates provides valuable insights into platform effectiveness. This data-driven approach allows you to refine your distribution strategy continually.

The eBook culminates with the concept of repurposing content. Different platforms demand different formats, and repurposing content allows you to reach a broader audience without reinventing the wheel. We provide strategies to adapt your content while maintaining its essence and message.

"Platform Selection: Navigating the Digital Landscape for Optimal Article Publishing and Distribution" transcends traditional guides—it's a transformative expedition through the crossroads of content and context. Whether you're a seasoned content creator looking to amplify your reach or a newcomer navigating the landscape of content distribution, this eBook equips you with the tools to select platforms strategically, ensuring your articles find their ideal readers. Join us on this immersive journey and unlock the full potential of platform selection, steering your content towards optimal visibility and engagement in the dynamic landscape of digital distribution.

Chapter <8>

Effective Outreach: Expanding Your Reach Through Influencer and Writer Collaboration

In the ever-expanding realm of content dissemination, effective outreach has become a pivotal key to unlocking wider audience engagement. **"Effective Outreach**: Expanding Your Reach Through Influencer and Writer Collaboration" invites you on a journey through the art and strategies of forging partnerships with influencers and fellow writers to amplify your content's reach and impact.

Understanding that collaboration is a catalyst for extending your content's sphere of influence, this exploration delves into the intricate dance of outreach, equipping you with insights and techniques to establish meaningful connections that resonate with both influencers and your target audience.

The journey begins by acknowledging the power of influencer collaboration. Influencers, with their established audiences and credibility, serve as conduits to new realms of engagement. We unveil the art of research, highlighting the importance of identifying influencers whose values and niches align seamlessly with your content.

Navigating deeper, the eBook delves into the significance of building authentic relationships. Influencer outreach is not merely transactional; it's about fostering genuine connections. Through real-world examples and expert insights, you'll uncover strategies to approach influencers with genuine interest and value proposition, creating partnerships that resonate on both sides.

Furthermore, the eBook explores the symbiotic nature of collaboration. Influencers benefit from fresh content and perspectives, while you gain access to their audience. We showcase how crafting content that aligns with an influencer's expertise and resonates with their followers enhances the potential for meaningful engagement.

The journey continues with the exploration of reciprocity. Establishing a relationship built on mutual benefit is essential. We delve into strategies to provide value to influencers, whether through guest posts, cross-promotion, or unique insights that enrich their content and engage their audience.

Moreover, the eBook unveils the concept of strategic alignment. An influencer's audience must align with your target readers for collaboration to be effective. We provide insights into assessing an influencer's audience demographics, interests, and engagement patterns, ensuring a match that maximises the reach of your content.

Intricately woven into the narrative is the concept of mutual amplification. Collaborative efforts extend beyond a single article or post. We explore strategies for sustaining the momentum through ongoing engagement, ensuring that both parties continue to benefit from the partnership.

The journey extends to the realm of fellow writers' collaboration. Co-authoring articles or conducting interviews with experts in your niche not only adds depth to your content but also widens your content's reach. We provide insights into identifying potential collaborators and structuring the collaboration for optimal engagement.

As the journey unfolds, we delve into the etiquette of outreach. Approaching influencers and fellow writers requires finesse and respect. We provide guidelines on crafting compelling outreach messages that communicate your intentions clearly and respectfully, increasing the likelihood of a positive response.

The eBook also highlights the significance of follow-up and relationship nurturing. Building a network of influencers and collaborators is an ongoing process. We offer insights into maintaining communication, expressing gratitude, and nurturing relationships for future collaborations.

Furthermore, the eBook showcases the role of social media in outreach. Engaging with influencers and fellow writers on social platforms builds familiarity and rapport. We provide strategies for meaningful interactions that lay the groundwork for deeper collaborations.

"Effective Outreach: Expanding Your Reach Through Influencer and Writer Collaboration" transcends conventional guides—it's a transformative expedition through the realms of networking, value exchange, and genuine connection. Whether you're a seasoned content creator seeking to amplify your influence or a newcomer navigating the landscape of collaboration, this eBook equips you with the tools to forge impactful partnerships that resonate with influencers and your audience alike. Join us on this immersive journey and unlock the full potential of effective outreach, extending your content's reach and impact in the dynamic landscape of digital engagement.

Chapter <9>

Visual Enhancement: Elevating Content Impact Through Strategic Visual Integration

In the ever-evolving landscape of content creation, the power of visual enhancement has emerged as a potent tool for conveying information and evoking emotions. **"Visual Enhancement:** Elevating Content Impact Through Strategic Visual Integration" takes you on a journey through the realm of incorporating visuals that not only amplify your content's impact but also enhance reader understanding and engagement.

Understanding that visuals are more than mere adornments—they are dynamic assets that enrich your content experience—this exploration delves into the art and science of weaving images, graphics, and multimedia seamlessly into your content, transforming it into a multi-dimensional and captivating narrative.

The journey begins by unveiling the cognitive allure of visuals. We explore the psychology behind why humans are drawn to images and how visuals enhance memory retention. Armed with this understanding, you'll recognize the potential of visuals to transcend language and resonate directly with your audience's emotions.

Navigating deeper, the eBook delves into the diverse world of visual formats. From images and infographics to videos and interactive elements, each format has its unique potential to engage. We showcase how to choose the right format for your content's purpose, ensuring a harmonious blend that reinforces your message.

Furthermore, the eBook explores the strategic integration of visuals. We highlight the importance of visuals that align with your content's narrative, offering insights into choosing images that complement your text and reinforce key points. When visuals and text work in tandem, they create a synergy that fosters understanding and impact.

The journey continues with the exploration of data visualisation. Infographics and charts distil complex data into comprehensible insights. We delve into techniques for transforming numbers and statistics into visuals that not only inform but also captivate, making data-driven content accessible and engaging.

Moreover, the eBook unveils the concept of storytelling through visuals. Visuals can convey narratives, emotions, and journeys. We explore how to craft a visual narrative that enhances your content, creating an immersive experience that resonates deeply with your readers.

Intricately woven into the narrative is the significance of visual consistency. Maintaining a consistent visual style across your content creates a recognizable brand identity. We provide insights into selecting colour schemes, fonts, and design elements that align with your brand and resonate with your audience.

The journey extends to the concept of accessibility. Inclusivity is paramount, and we showcase how to make your visuals accessible to all readers, including those with visual impairments. Strategies such as alt text and captions ensure that everyone can engage with your content fully.

As the journey unfolds, we delve into the synergy between visuals and social media. Social platforms thrive on visual content, and we offer insights into tailoring your visuals for maximum impact on platforms like Instagram, Pinterest, and LinkedIn.

The eBook also highlights the role of multimedia. Videos, podcasts, and animations provide a dynamic layer to your content. We showcase how incorporating multimedia elements can transform your content into a multi-sensory experience that captures attention and fosters engagement.

Furthermore, the eBook underscores the importance of testing and optimization. Different visuals resonate differently with various audiences. We delve into strategies for A/B testing visuals to gauge their impact and refine your visual strategy over time.

"Visual Enhancement: Elevating Content Impact Through Strategic Visual Integration" transcends conventional guides—it's a transformative expedition into the realm of visual storytelling and engagement. Whether you're a seasoned content creator seeking to enrich your approach or a newcomer navigating the landscape of visual integration, this eBook equips you with the tools to craft content that resonates through visual narratives. Join us on this immersive journey and unlock the full potential of visual enhancement, elevating your content's impact and understanding in the dynamic landscape of digital engagement.

Chapter <10>

Social Media Integration: Harnessing Social Platforms for Amplified Article Promotion and Sharing

In the interconnected realm of digital communication, the art of social media integration has emerged as a dynamic force for propelling content to new heights of visibility and engagement. **"Social Media Integration:** Harnessing Social Platforms for Amplified Article Promotion and Sharing" takes you on a journey through the intricacies of leveraging social media to promote and share your articles, enabling your content to resonate with a wider audience and foster meaningful connections.

Understanding that social media is a powerful conduit for content dissemination, this exploration delves into the strategies and insights that drive effective social media integration. You'll be equipped to navigate the vibrant landscape of social platforms and harness their potential to amplify your content's reach and impact.

The journey begins by acknowledging the multifaceted appeal of social media. From Facebook to Twitter, Instagram to LinkedIn, each platform boasts its unique audience and engagement dynamics. We unveil the art of understanding your target audience's social media preferences, ensuring that your content resonates where it matters most.

Navigating deeper, the eBook delves into the significance of content adaptation. Every platform has its own format, tone, and audience behaviour. We showcase how to tailor your articles for each platform, adapting your content to suit the platform's style and strengths, thereby maximising its appeal and shareability.

Furthermore, the eBook explores the concept of strategic timing. The lifespan of a social media post varies across platforms. We provide insights into when to share your articles for optimal engagement, ensuring that your content reaches its audience when they're most active and receptive.

The journey continues with the exploration of engagement dynamics. Social media is a two-way street, and we delve into strategies to foster interactions with your audience. Responding to comments, initiating discussions, and actively engaging with your readers create a sense of community around your content.

Moreover, the eBook unveils the power of visual storytelling on social platforms. Images, videos, and infographics are highly shareable and engaging. We provide insights into creating visuals that encapsulate your article's essence and evoke curiosity, prompting users to explore your content further.

Intricately woven into the narrative is the concept of consistency. Maintaining an active presence on social media requires consistent posting and engagement. We showcase how to craft a content calendar that aligns with each platform's nuances, ensuring a steady stream of content that sustains engagement.

The journey extends to the concept of cross-promotion. Collaborating with other content creators or influencers allows you to tap into new audiences and extend your content's reach. We provide strategies for mutually beneficial partnerships that broaden your content's exposure.

As the journey unfolds, we delve into the role of hashtags. These seemingly innocuous symbols are potent tools for increasing discoverability. We explore strategies for selecting relevant and trending hashtags that amplify the visibility of your content.

The eBook also highlights the significance of analytics. Social media platforms offer insights into post performance, audience engagement, and reach. We provide insights into interpreting these metrics to refine your social media strategy continually.

Furthermore, the eBook underscores the importance of authenticity. Social media users value transparency and genuine connections. We offer insights into crafting posts that reflect your voice and values, fostering a relatable and lasting connection with your audience.

"Social Media Integration: Harnessing Social Platforms for Amplified Article Promotion and Sharing" transcends conventional guides—it's a transformative expedition into the realm of audience engagement and connection. Whether you're a seasoned content creator seeking to expand your influence or a newcomer navigating the landscape of social media promotion, this eBook equips you with the tools to integrate your content seamlessly with social platforms. Join us on this immersive journey and unlock the full potential of social media integration, magnifying your content's reach and impact in the dynamic landscape of digital engagement.

Chapter <11>

Analytics Utilisation: Empowering Data-Driven Article Marketing Strategies for Optimal Impact

In the data-driven realm of digital marketing, the art of analytics utilisation has risen as a pivotal force for refining strategies and elevating content's impact. "Analytics Utilisation: Empowering Data-Driven Article Marketing Strategies for Optimal Impact" embarks on a journey through the dynamic landscape of harnessing data to refine your article marketing approach, enabling you to make informed decisions and achieve meaningful results.

Understanding that insights derived from analytics have the power to shape, refine, and amplify your content strategies, this exploration delves into the strategies and techniques that empower you to unlock the full potential of data-driven marketing.

The journey begins by unveiling the significance of data-driven decision-making. Analytics provide a lens through which you can gain insights into your audience's behaviour, preferences, and interactions. We explore how embracing data allows you to optimise your article marketing approach by understanding what resonates and what needs adjustment.

Navigating deeper, the eBook delves into the diverse world of analytics tools. From Google Analytics to social media insights, each platform offers a wealth of data that can illuminate your marketing journey. We showcase how to leverage these tools to track key metrics, measure engagement, and gain a comprehensive view of your content's performance.

Furthermore, the eBook explores the art of goal setting. By defining clear objectives for your article marketing campaigns, you can measure success against concrete benchmarks. We provide insights into crafting SMART (Specific, Measurable, Achievable, Relevant, Time-bound) goals that guide your data analysis effectively.

The journey continues with the exploration of audience insights. Analytics provide valuable data about your readers—demographics, interests, location, and behaviour patterns. We delve into strategies for translating these insights into actionable steps that refine your content's relevance and resonance.

Moreover, the eBook unveils the concept of content performance analysis. We showcase how to dissect metrics such as page views, time on page, bounce rates, and click-through rates to evaluate how your content is being consumed and where potential improvements lie.

Intricately woven into the narrative is the significance of A/B testing. This data-driven technique allows you to compare different variables—such as headlines, visuals, or calls to action—to determine what performs best. We offer insights into conducting effective A/B tests that lead to refined content strategies.

The journey extends to the concept of social media analytics. Social platforms provide data on post reach, engagement, and audience demographics. We explore how to interpret these metrics to tailor your social media strategies and amplify your content's reach.

As the journey unfolds, we delve into the synergy between analytics and SEO. Understanding which keywords drive organic traffic and how users find your content empowers you to optimise your content for better search engine visibility.

The eBook also highlights the role of audience engagement metrics. Comments, shares, and interactions reflect how your content resonates with readers. We provide insights into interpreting these metrics to gauge audience sentiment and adjust your approach accordingly.

Furthermore, the eBook underscores the importance of iteration. Data-driven marketing is an ongoing process of refinement. We offer insights into continuously monitoring metrics, adapting strategies, and testing new approaches to ensure lasting success.

The journey culminates with the concept of ROI analysis. By assessing the return on investment for your article marketing efforts, you can determine which strategies yield the best results. We provide insights into measuring both quantitative and qualitative returns to gain a comprehensive perspective.

"**Analytics Utilisation:** Empowering Data-Driven Article Marketing Strategies for Optimal Impact" transcends conventional guides—it's a transformative expedition into the realm of insights and optimization. Whether you're a seasoned marketer seeking to elevate your approach or a newcomer navigating the landscape of data-driven marketing, this eBook equips you with the tools to harness analytics for refining your article marketing strategies. Join us on this immersive journey and unlock the full potential of data-driven decision-making, shaping impactful content strategies in the dynamic landscape of digital marketing.

Chapter <12>

Building Credibility: Establishing Niche Authority Through Insightful and Researched Articles

In the vast expanse of digital content, building credibility has emerged as a foundational cornerstone for establishing oneself as a trusted authority in a specific niche. **"Building Credibility:** Establishing Niche Authority Through Insightful and Researched Articles" embarks on a journey through the art and strategies of cultivating credibility by crafting articles that not only resonate with your target audience but also position you as an expert in your field.

Understanding that credibility is the currency of trust and influence, this exploration delves into the process of creating articles that not only inform but also inspire confidence, fostering connections that go beyond superficial engagement.

The journey begins by unveiling the essence of credibility. Credibility isn't merely about demonstrating expertise; it's about showcasing a deep understanding of your niche. We explore how well-researched and insightful articles serve as the foundation for establishing trust and resonance with your audience.

Navigating deeper, the eBook delves into the significance of in-depth research. Well-researched articles reflect your commitment to providing accurate and valuable information. We showcase how to approach research strategically, curating authoritative sources that lend weight to your insights and arguments.

Furthermore, the eBook explores the power of original insights. While research is essential, presenting fresh perspectives and unique viewpoints elevates your credibility. We provide insights into fostering creativity within your niche, offering readers insights they may not find elsewhere.

The journey continues with the exploration of quality over quantity. In the digital age, the sheer volume of content can dilute its impact. We delve into strategies for producing fewer articles of higher quality, each packed with valuable insights that showcase your expertise.

Moreover, the eBook unveils the significance of clarity and structure. Well-structured articles enhance readability and comprehension. We provide insights into crafting introductions that grab attention, body sections that provide value, and conclusions that leave a lasting impression.

Intricately woven into the narrative is the concept of citing sources. References and citations not only lend credibility to your claims but also provide readers with avenues for further exploration. We offer guidance on proper citation practices that enhance your article's authenticity.

The journey extends to the concept of engagement. Credibility is built not just through the content itself, but also through interactions with your audience. We explore strategies for responding to comments, addressing questions, and nurturing discussions around your articles.

As the journey unfolds, we delve into the synergy between storytelling and credibility. Stories humanise your content, making it relatable and memorable. We provide insights into incorporating anecdotes, case studies, and personal experiences that resonate with readers on both an intellectual and emotional level.

The eBook also highlights the role of consistency. Regularly delivering well-researched and insightful articles builds anticipation and trust among your audience. We offer insights into maintaining a consistent publishing schedule that aligns with your audience's expectations.

Furthermore, the eBook underscores the importance of authenticity. Credibility is closely tied to authenticity. We explore how injecting your unique voice and personality into your articles fosters a sense of connection and relatability with your audience.

The journey culminates with the concept of continuous learning. Niche authority isn't static; it requires ongoing education and adaptation. We provide insights into staying updated with industry trends, new research, and evolving perspectives to maintain your credibility over time.

"Building Credibility: Establishing Niche Authority Through Insightful and Researched Articles" transcends conventional guides—it's a transformative expedition into the realm of trust, expertise, and meaningful engagement. Whether you're a seasoned authority seeking to refine your approach or a newcomer navigating the landscape of credibility-building, this eBook equips you with the tools to create articles that resonate deeply and position you as a respected expert in your niche. Join us on this immersive journey and unlock the full potential of building credibility through insightful content in the dynamic landscape of digital expertise.

Chapter <13>

Long-Term Engagement: Fostering Lasting Connections Through Consistent Value Delivery

In the ever-evolving realm of digital content, the art of long-term engagement has emerged as a linchpin for cultivating a loyal readership that transcends fleeting interactions. **"Long-Term Engagement:** Fostering Lasting Connections Through Consistent Value Delivery" embarks on a journey through the strategies and techniques that empower you to create articles that not only resonate with your audience but also establish a meaningful and enduring relationship.

Understanding that building lasting connections requires a commitment to consistently delivering value, this exploration delves into the process of crafting articles that not only capture attention but also nurture sustained engagement and loyalty.

The journey begins by unveiling the essence of long-term engagement. Beyond immediate interactions, it's about fostering a sense of connection that prompts readers to return for more. We explore how articles that consistently deliver value are the cornerstone of this enduring relationship.

Navigating deeper, the eBook delves into the significance of understanding your audience. Long-term engagement is rooted in addressing your readers' evolving needs and preferences. We showcase how to listen to your audience, gather feedback, and adjust your content strategy accordingly.

Furthermore, the eBook explores the power of consistent value delivery. Each article should provide insights, solutions, or inspiration that enriches your readers' lives. We provide insights into crafting content that goes beyond superficial engagement, leaving a lasting impact.

The journey continues with the exploration of thematic continuity. Connecting articles under common themes or series enhances the sense of anticipation and connection. We offer strategies for curating thematic content that guides readers on a journey of exploration and learning.

Moreover, the eBook unveils the significance of relatability. Readers engage more deeply when they can see themselves in your content. We explore how to weave personal anecdotes, experiences, and relatable stories into your articles to create a sense of shared understanding.

Intricately woven into the narrative is the concept of ongoing learning. Articles that delve into industry trends, insights, and developments keep your readers informed and engaged. We provide insights into staying updated and curating content that reflects the latest advancements.

The journey extends to the concept of interactivity. Engaging your readers through polls, quizzes, comments, and discussions makes them feel like active participants in your content journey. We showcase how to foster interactive experiences that deepen engagement.

As the journey unfolds, we delve into the synergy between multimedia and long-term engagement. Incorporating videos, podcasts, and infographics adds variety and depth to your content. We offer insights into how multimedia elements enrich your readers' experience.

The eBook also highlights the role of feedback loops. Actively seeking feedback and incorporating reader suggestions not only enhances your content but also nurtures a sense of community. We provide strategies for creating open channels of communication with your audience.

Furthermore, the eBook underscores the importance of authenticity. Long-term engagement is built on trust, and authenticity is a foundational element of trust. We explore how being genuine, transparent, and true to your values fosters a deeper connection with your readers.

The journey culminates with the concept of adaptability. Audience preferences and trends evolve over time. We provide insights into the art of adapting your content strategy while staying true to your core values, ensuring continued resonance with your readers.

"Long-Term Engagement: Fostering Lasting Connections Through Consistent Value Delivery" transcends conventional guides—it's a transformative expedition into the realm of lasting impact, connection, and loyalty. Whether you're a seasoned content creator seeking to deepen your engagement or a newcomer navigating the landscape of sustained relationships, this eBook equips you with the tools to create articles that resonate beyond the moment, fostering a loyal readership in the dynamic landscape of digital connections. Join us on this immersive journey and unlock the full potential of long-term engagement, cultivating meaningful and lasting relationships through your content.

Chapter <14>

SEO Mastery: Elevating Your Articles' Visibility Through Advanced Search Engine Optimization Techniques

In the ever-evolving realm of digital content, SEO mastery has emerged as a potent force for catapulting articles to the forefront of search engine results. "**SEO Mastery:** Elevating Your Articles' Visibility Through Advanced Search Engine Optimization Techniques" embarks on a journey through the intricacies of implementing advanced SEO strategies that not only enhance your articles' visibility but also position them for maximum impact in search engine rankings.

Understanding that visibility in search engines is a gateway to audience engagement, this exploration delves into the art and science of crafting articles that resonate with both readers and search algorithms, propelling your content to the eyes of those seeking your insights.

The journey begins by unveiling the essence of advanced SEO. It's not just about keywords; it's about understanding search intent and providing the most relevant content. We explore how advanced SEO techniques involve a holistic approach that blends technical optimization with reader-centric content creation.

Navigating deeper, the eBook delves into the significance of keyword research. Advanced SEO requires understanding your audience's search queries and tailoring your content to meet those needs. We showcase how to identify long-tail keywords, analyse search volumes, and uncover valuable keyword opportunities.

Furthermore, the eBook explores the power of semantic SEO. Search engines have evolved to understand context and meaning. We provide insights into crafting content that uses synonyms, related terms, and natural language to signal relevance to search engines.

The journey continues with the exploration of technical SEO. Page speed, mobile responsiveness, and structured data are integral factors in modern

SEO. We offer strategies for optimising your website's technical aspects to provide a seamless experience for users and search engines alike.

Moreover, the eBook unveils the significance of content structure. Well-organised content not only engages readers but also signals to search engines that your content is valuable. We provide insights into creating clear headings, subheadings, and a logical flow that enhances both readability and search visibility.

Intricately woven into the narrative is the concept of backlink building. High-quality backlinks are a testament to your content's authority. We explore strategies for earning authoritative and relevant backlinks that enhance your content's credibility in the eyes of search engines.

The journey extends to the concept of user experience. A positive user experience contributes to lower bounce rates and higher engagement, both of which are important ranking factors. We offer insights into creating intuitive navigation, engaging visuals, and responsive design that enhance user satisfaction.

As the journey unfolds, we delve into the synergy between multimedia and SEO. Videos, images, and other multimedia elements enrich your content and keep readers engaged. We showcase how optimising these elements contributes to both user experience and search engine visibility.

The eBook also highlights the role of local SEO. If you have a physical presence, optimising for local searches is crucial. We provide insights into claiming your Google My Business listing, generating reviews, and utilising location-specific keywords.

Furthermore, the eBook underscores the importance of analytics. Monitoring SEO metrics like organic traffic, click-through rates, and bounce rates provides insights into your content's performance. We offer guidance on interpreting these metrics to refine your SEO strategy continually.

The journey culminates with the concept of continuous learning. SEO algorithms evolve, and staying updated with industry trends is essential. We provide insights into reputable sources for SEO news and updates to ensure your strategies remain effective.

"SEO Mastery: Elevating Your Articles' Visibility Through Advanced Search Engine Optimization Techniques" transcends conventional guides—it's a transformative expedition into the realm of search algorithms, user intent, and content resonance. Whether you're a seasoned content creator seeking to amplify your reach or a newcomer navigating the landscape of advanced SEO, this eBook equips you with the tools to optimize your articles for search engines and readers alike. Join us on this immersive journey and unlock the full potential of advanced SEO, propelling your content to the forefront of search engine visibility in the dynamic landscape of digital discovery.

Chapter <15>

Measuring Success: Navigating the Metrics Landscape for Data-Driven Article Marketing Enhancement

In the ever-evolving world of digital marketing, measuring success has emerged as a guiding light to steer article marketing strategies towards optimal outcomes. "Measuring Success: Navigating the Metrics Landscape for Data-Driven Article Marketing Enhancement" embarks on a journey through the realm of metrics, equipping you with the tools and insights needed to gauge the effectiveness of your article marketing efforts and make data-driven improvements.

Understanding that success is not a singular achievement but an ongoing process of refinement, this exploration delves into the art of deciphering metrics, translating them into actionable insights, and adapting your strategies for impactful results.

The journey begins by unveiling the essence of metrics-driven enhancement. Beyond the surface metrics, it's about understanding what resonates with your audience and fine-tuning your approach accordingly. We explore how metrics provide a roadmap for continuous improvement and growth.

Navigating deeper, the eBook delves into the significance of defining success metrics. Success varies based on your goals—whether it's increased website traffic, higher engagement, or improved conversion rates. We showcase how to set clear and measurable goals that guide your metrics analysis.

Furthermore, the eBook explores the power of traffic metrics. Pageviews, unique visitors, and time on page offer insights into your content's reach and engagement. We provide strategies for interpreting these metrics to understand which articles resonate most with your audience.

The journey continues with the exploration of engagement metrics. Metrics like comments, shares, and click-through rates reflect how deeply your content resonates with readers. We offer insights into assessing engagement metrics to identify content that sparks meaningful interactions.

Moreover, the eBook unveils the significance of conversion metrics. If your goal is to drive specific actions—such as sign-ups, downloads, or purchases—conversion metrics are key. We provide insights into tracking conversion rates, assessing landing page effectiveness, and optimising calls to action.

Intricately woven into the narrative is the concept of audience insights. Metrics offer valuable data about your readers—demographics, location, interests, and behaviour patterns. We explore how to use this data to tailor your content and strategies to meet their needs.

The journey extends to the concept of referral metrics. Knowing where your traffic comes from—search engines, social media, direct visits—provides insights into your content's discoverability and distribution. We offer strategies for optimising your content promotion based on referral sources.

As the journey unfolds, we delve into the synergy between metrics and content optimization. Metrics reveal which topics and formats resonate most. We showcase how to use this information to refine your content strategy, creating articles that align with audience preferences.

The eBook also highlights the role of testing and experimentation. A/B testing headlines, visuals, and other elements provides insights into what works best. We provide insights into structuring effective tests and using the results to iterate on your strategies.

Furthermore, the eBook underscores the importance of the feedback loop. Metrics analysis is not a one-time event; it's an ongoing process. We offer guidance on regularly reviewing metrics, identifying trends, and adapting your strategies to stay aligned with your goals.

The journey culminates with the concept of holistic assessment. Success isn't confined to a single metric; it's the culmination of multiple factors. We provide insights into creating a balanced scorecard that considers a range of metrics to provide a comprehensive view of your article marketing effectiveness.

"**Measuring Success:** Navigating the Metrics Landscape for Data-Driven Article Marketing Enhancement" transcends conventional guides—it's a transformative expedition into the realm of insights, adaptability, and refinement. Whether you're a seasoned marketer seeking to elevate your approach or a newcomer navigating the landscape of metrics analysis, this eBook equips you with the tools to gauge the effectiveness of your article marketing efforts. Join us on this immersive journey and unlock the full potential of metrics-driven improvement, steering your content strategies towards impactful results in the dynamic landscape of digital marketing.